FLESHLY DATE
OR
GODLY MATE

Mary Lee Vance

Fleshly Date or Godly Mate
Copyright ©2019 Mary Lee Vance
January 2019

Lifted Publishing
Atlanta, Georgia

ISBN-13: 978-0578215365
ISBN-10: 0578215365

Edited by: C. A. McKenzie
Cover Artist: B. Singh

LIFTED
PUBLISHING

Contents

Introduction

Girl, he is so fine! He's tall, muscular, and has everything that I want in man going for himself. He has a great job with great benefits. He's a great family man. He's respectful, opens car doors for me, pays for my dates, always makes time for me. This, for sure, is the man I will marry, right?

Women have been told to write a list of all the things they want in a man, but do the characteristics listed feed your flesh or your future? Some of us put our trust in everything God has for us except finding the perfect mate. Why is that?

This book is designed to help you distinguish the difference between your fleshly desires and your Godly desires when it comes to choosing a mate. I will use biblical references to help and guide you to freedom, use realistic examples of the bumps and bruises down the road of my own path, and show how God revealed to me my husband.

I was, of course, not perfect and messed up along the way, but His sufficient grace saved me, and it can save you, too! I want to reach all women, no matter where they are, to help align them with God and the path He has for them.

SURELY IT'S MEANT FOR YOUR FUTURE PROSPEROUS LIFE! (Jeremiah 29:11, New Living Translation).

Chapter 1

What Is Your Flesh?

In December 2014, fresh out of college, I moved to Atlanta, Georgia. I took a giant leap of faith and left my entire family in California, where I was born and raised. I had just gotten out of a three-year relationship and engagement, and I was starting fresh, brand new. I was ready to date and find my husband.

I, of course, had my list. Number one on the list was a man chasing after God's own heart. I thought this was written clearly enough that God would understand exactly what I was asking for. I had my physical attributes, as well, and there was not going to be any substitutions. He had to be taller than I was. He had to be cute, muscular, from a good family, and keep me mentally stimulated.

So I went on the prowl, which was my first mistake—myself looking for a man. Why? *Because a man who finds a wife, finds a good thing, and obtains favor from the Lord* (Proverbs 18:22). I wasn't thinking about these verses. I was focused on finding my husband because I wanted him now!

I joined dating websites and went on blind dates my friends set up for me. I was desperate for my husband. I looked high, low, in the desert, and in the valley. I received the attention I wanted but not the attention I needed.

At all of my dates, I asked these two simple questions: "Do you know Jesus?" and "Do you actively serve in your church?" I asked the right questions and accepted the wrong answer of, "Yes, I know who Jesus is, but I don't go to church." I still dated them and conversed with them because I wanted a mate.

I told my mother about a particular guy, with whom I had so much fun that I thought he was the one. He had a good job, took me on dates, and went the extra mile to put a smile on my face every day, but he lacked spiritually. There I was, creating soul ties with a dead person who had no intention to follow Christ, but my first expectation was a man chasing after God's own heart? Was I dead, as well? (Ephesians 2:1).

I faithfully attended church on Sundays and Bible study on Tuesday, but spiritually I was dead because I was following after the dead. I was enticed by the dead and liked how the dead made me feel. I felt special. He knew what to say and when to say it. He knew where to touch me and manipulate me to agree to engage in intercourse without the intention of even viewing me as his wife. I enjoyed my sinful nature (I Corinthians 7:2).

It was rough for a while because I kept choosing my own way. I didn't trust that God was able to give me the desires of my heart, but I couldn't even give me what my own heart desired, either. I still decided to lean on my own understanding. I didn't trust His will, but I constantly chose to trust my ever-failing flesh. I allowed my flesh to choose who was right for me, and I didn't have time for the God-chosen one. I was desperate for a husband, and at that point, my way was better than God's will.

What does flesh mean? I want to make sure to give you the spiritual definition of what it is to act in our flesh rather than our spirit. In Romans 7:5, "When *we are controlled by our flesh (old nature), sinful desires are at work within us, and the law arouses these evil desires that produces a harvest of sinful deeds, resulting in death,*" which means we have a battle between the spirit that God gives us and the fleshly spirit of sin that we were born into. When we act in our flesh, we produce unfulfilling desires, broken hearts, disappointment, rejection, and inconsistency. We are unequally yoked, and we question why these relationships entered into without the Holy Spirit guiding us reach dead ends.

I can look back and say that I completely operated in my flesh and hit a lot of dead ends when depending on my flesh rather than the Holy Spirit. In the end, I discovered the Holy Spirit was leading me the whole time, and I ignored Him.

Chapter 2

Test Drive Your Soul Tie

Society tells us today that we must see what a man is working with before we engage or even think about marrying him or being with him. We must make sure his intercourse is better than anything we have ever expected because if we wait, we may be disappointed, right? So we give ourselves away, man after man after man, and wonder why we are still emotionally connected to men when we are no longer in contact with them. We want to contact them to see how they are doing, and we find ourselves on their social media sites, reminiscing about the past, what it was, and what could have been. Or we simply listen to false promises that he so gently speaks in your ear.

On that first night, he is already talking about spending the rest of his life with you. We see women celebrities who flaunt their sexuality as if it is okay to sleep with all the men in the world, but they fail to see how valuable they are.

Intercourse with an individual is defined as "physical sexual contact between individuals." God speaks directly in Corinthians about becoming one flesh with someone who is not your wife or husband. He states in Corinthians 6:16-18 NLT, *"And don't you* realize that if a man joins himself to a prostitute, he becomes one body with her? For the Scriptures say, 'The two are united into one'. But the person who is joined to the Lord is one spirit with him. Run from sexual sin! No other sin so clearly affects the body as this one does. For sexual immorality is a sin against your own body."

I know for sure that every man with whom we have physical intercourse does not make us one with God. The Scripture states that once we are in our flesh and enter into sexual immortality, we enter into a bond or soul tie with a man that God has not called us to pair with. He says we should avoid sin at all cost, but sexual sin affects the body. Sex feels good, and sometimes we just want to feel good. Honestly, are those two to three minutes' worth losing the promise that God has given you?

God tells us in Acts 15:29 that *"You must abstain from...sexual immorality. If you do this, you will prosper."* I don't know about you, but what I do know for sure is that I would love to live the prosperous life God has for me. The sad thing is that we see celebrities every day with low to no morals who flaunt sexual immorality as if they are living their best lives, but the majority of them are not in marriages and promote their impure lives as if it's acceptable to God.

In the shows and movies, we see husbands cheating on wives or vice versa, and we see that divorce is always an option. We rarely have the good examples of what a strong Christian marriage looks like because it is not popular. It is said that it is simply too hard to live a righteous life, so we take the easy route.

There is a lack of discipline in our lives. We invite the enemy to run rampant and then we spiral out of control. We wonder why things can't go right. At least, that's happened to me, but we never wanted to change; we wanted to continue to do things the way that we wanted to do them.

I was the woman that was like, *Ehhh, I don't know if I could marry you if you did not have all of my check marks crossed off the list.* I kept insisting that the man I marry must love God and trust Him when I didn't love God. I was unsure at that point in my life if I even loved myself. I gave myself away to men, test-driving to see if they were the whole package, not trusting that God can direct my life, enjoyment, and fullness. I didn't trust that God knew my exact needs and would give me exceeding and abundantly. I didn't trust that if I just asked Him for it and truly believed in my heart that I received it, he would make it happen in the earthly realm. I didn't believe the one and true promise keeper. I was disobedient, and I was unfaithful to my relationship with my heavenly Father.

There was one particular man I continually entertained. I was introduced to him by a then close coworker. The first month or so, he said all the right things. I received morning texts, texts throughout the day, random phone calls, amazing dates, and yes, I engaged in sex. He was divorced with two kids. I thought he was the one because he showed me to the world. He had a six-figure salary and rented nice vehicles to take me out on dates. But he had had a dealing with the law and was on probation, and he drank a lot.

Red flags! Stop signs! Nope, I didn't pay attention to any of those flags in the beginning because he was feeding my flesh with a temporary void that I did not allow Jesus to fill. After a month of putting up a good front, everything started to fade quickly. We argued as if we had been in a relationship for years. He had no intention to stop drinking. He went to his mother's church every so often, but did he live a holy and righteous life? Negative. But I thought he was the best I was going to get.

I put in overtime with this man. I bought him a nice watch, expensive cologne, outfits for his children. I even prayed over him so God could fix him. I thought if he was around me enough that he would change. It got worse and not for the better, and I kept giving myself away to this man and started to feel what he felt—sadness, anger, depression. I was upset that nothing ever went right, that I was not adequate to feel loved. I was one flesh with this man, and he was nowhere near the ideal man of God that I had asked for. I settled for someone who didn't value me because I didn't value myself. What put the icing on the cake was that he ended up dating the coworker who had introduced us. How foolish could I have been? He lacked self-love, values, morals, and self-esteem, and I allowed all of those spirits to enter my body because I had intercourse with someone God did not intend to be my desired husband

As I write this, I feel convicted all over again. I knew what I was doing was not of God, but I continued to follow my sinful nature believing it would lead me to my husband. I created an even bigger problem for myself and became depressed. No one wanted to spend their life with me, so what was wrong with me? Why was I not worth these men staying in my life to have a real relationship? Why did all of these end up being one-night stands after talking for a few weeks and then the men disappearing? What was wrong with me?

I caused problems for myself that I did not necessarily have to have if I had followed the Holy Spirit and not my sinful nature. When I first arrived in Atlanta, I was sexually impure for about six months until I hit my head hard enough on one of God's stop signs and sank to my lowest. I had given myself away to all of these men, and none of them were anywhere close to being my husband.

I spent a lot of time working on myself for a good six months. I cried through the process, wondering where my husband was and why he hadn't found me. But at the same time, God had to break me down in order to build me back up. He had to help me understand my worth, and we had to establish trust.

Chapter 3

Do You Really Trust God?

I sometimes have had a hard time trusting God in some areas of my life. I trusted Him with my finances, I trusted He would keep me in times of trouble, I trusted I would make it through difficult times as long as I kept Him first, but I didn't trust that He would be able to pick the right mate.

I knew the verses of the different promises God has for us. I declared them over my life to try to break the cycle. I had verses at my desk at work as a constant reminder. I had Jeremiah 29:11: *"For I know the plans I have for you declares the LORD. 'They are plans for good and not for disaster, to give you a future and a hope.'"* I also had John 10:10: *"The thief's purpose is to steal and kill and destroy. My purpose is to give them a rich and satisfying life."* My favorite is Psalms 37:4: *"Take delight in the Lord, and he will give you your heart's desire."*

I misinterpreted the whole Scripture. I clearly skipped over the "taking delight in the Lord" part and thought that the Lord was going to give me my heart's desire. Wrong! My heart was not aligned to what His Word stated, and I was pleading with God and did not know the extent of what His delightedness truly was.

I went along thinking that God was in some small box and skipped over my requests, not caring about my tears. I started to doubt how powerful God was. At that point, I didn't care about all the miracles He had done. I was frustrated why He couldn't fulfill my request on my time. I used to pray, "I trust you, Lord," and then turn around and say, "Maybe God can't hear me" to "Because I have sinned, I will never have the man I asked God for." Partial trust, which is distrust all together. You either trust God or you don't.

I saw everyone around me become engaged or get married, and I had to act as if I was happy for them. Really, I was asking God why He showed everyone around me this blessing that I had been in desperate need of. I was mad at God and had temper tantrums, spitting His promises back in His face and calling Him a liar for not being able to produce my husband on my time.

I wrote my list over and over again, changing it to what satisfied my flesh more than my spirit. I settled, thinking maybe he didn't have to have a heart chasing after God and could just know the realm of who Jesus was. I felt my expectations were too high, and at that point, I didn't trust God could succeed with my expectations.

God forced me to trust Him. There was definitely turbulence along the way. He stripped away every man I placed before Him, and He got me to a point where I was by myself so I could face that I was giving myself away and wasting time with men who don't have a heart similar to His. He had me deal with my insecurities. He had me deal with my negative thoughts about myself, as well as my negative thoughts of Him. He had to mold and fix my heart. He had to empty out my flesh and pour His spirit onto me.

Chapter 4

Work Out Your Kinks

Sexual Immorality

Galatians 5:16-17 states, *"So I say, let the Holy spirit guide your lives. Then you won't be doing what your sinful nature craves. The sinful nature wants to do evil, which just the opposite of what the Spirit wants. And the Spirit gives us the desires that are opposite of what the sinful nature desires. These two forces are constantly fighting each other, so you are not free to carry out your good intentions."*

My intentions were good, but my flesh did not produce anything fruitful. When I read Galatians for the first time, my whole life was in complete and utter shock. I didn't know Jesus was going to hit me upside the head so hard. I knew half of the things listed in these Scriptures I participated in or was still currently enslaved to at that time.

The Bible also speaks to what our sinful natures enslave us to when we don't adhere to the Holy Spirit. Galatians 5:19 states, *"When you follow the desires of your sinful nature, the results are very clear: sexual immorality, impurity, lustful pleasures, idolatry, sorcery, hostility, quarreling, jealousy, outbursts of anger, selfish ambition, dissension, division, envy, drunkenness, wild parties, and other sins like these. Let me tell you again, as I have before, that anyone living that sort of life will not inherit the Kingdom of God."*

I knew for sure that I definitely had something I needed help with. I was sexually immoral, I was impure, I had a lot of lustful desires, I was hostile, I loved a great argument, I had jealousy issues, I would outburst with anger due to frustration, I envied other women and their marriages, and I may have had a little bit of self-ambition. What made me scared the most was that if I continued to live the life I was living, I was not going to inherit the Kingdom of God, and not doing that was not an option.

We, as women, sometimes struggle with a lot of those situations that I mentioned above. I want you to receive freedom today! I want to show you where there is healing in the Word for our shortcomings and how we can find wholeness within ourselves.

Growing up, I was told I shouldn't have sex and that it was a sin, but it was never explained to me biblically why God wants us to abstain from being impure, having sexual immorality and lustful desires. I became sexually active at sixteen years old. My naive self didn't understand what "keeping herself" was all about.

Colossians 3:5 says: *"So put to death the sinful, earthy things lurking within you. Have nothing to do with sexual immorality,* impurity, lust, and evil desires. Don't be greedy, for a greedy person is an idolater, worshiping the things of this world." Putting to death, of course, means killing that desire or getting rid of that desire if it is outside of marriage. In Act 15:29 He states if we abstain from sexual immorality that we will do well. Not only that, there is forgiveness. God wants to forgive your past so that you can live in freedom in His Spirit that lives within you.

1 John 1: 9 states, *"But if we confess our sins to Him, He is faithful and just to forgive us our sins and to cleanse us from all wickedness."* There is healing in that statement. Go ahead and write down all your faults when it comes to sexual sin. You can simply say:

"God, I want to live for you and be about your business,
I confess ___ with ____, and I ask that you forgive me, Lord.
Not only forgive me, Lord, but cleanse me of my past so that
I never return there, renew my mind, and renew my focus that
I am able to chase after You with my whole heart and focus
on the things you want me to focus on and help me, God. Help
me to be the woman of God that you have created me to be.
In Jesus' Name, Amen."

Hostility and Quarreling

Another issue we deal with is hostility. We are hostile with family, friends, spouses. We are hostile in uncomfortable situations and dealing with unusual circumstances.

The definition of hostile is being unfriendly and antagonistic. Some synonyms of hostile are: unkind, bitter, unsympathetic, malicious, vicious, poisonous, aggressive, confrontational, and belligerent. Romans 8:7 states, *"For the sinful nature is always hostile to God. It never did obey God's laws, and it never will."*

There were many times I became hostile with God for not giving me the things I wanted. My hostility with God is a spirit I carried with me and it poured onto all those around me. I would be unkind with a particular man I was dating because every time I talked about marriage or mentioned desiring to be a wife and have children, he would say, "I don't plan on remarrying or having any more kids." I became hostile while dating when men told me I was fat or ugly or that I would never have a husband. I was even hostile with people in general, some of whom were down-right rude. The sad part is I actually started to believe those horrific things that were said to me. Yes, I became bitter and unkind and had every reason why I should "clap back." I was always on defense because hearing the things people thought about me gave me a negative impact on how I felt about myself. I did not have any knowledge about how God saw me because I was not disciplined in the Bible to know. I had no clue how precious I was to God.

Have you ever argued your point until your face turned blue? Yeah, that was me. I remember quarreling with this guy about marriage. He did not understand the importance of marriage. He had no intentions of marriage but wanted a forever exclusive relationship with all the benefits. I knew the Word of God advised otherwise, and yet I still wanted his company, his affection, his shallow love, and his attention. I argued about the smallest things, not even understanding why I was upset or if it was even worth being uptight about.

I got to the point of belittling men, tearing down their self-esteem even if they didn't say anything unkind to me. I had a brash harshness that if your feelings were hurt then maybe you shouldn't be immature. I didn't see the depth of how I said things and how they came off. I snapped if I was reminded of my past hurt or if things didn't go my way. I took it upon myself to seek revenge.

There was nothing meek about my spirit. I could not control my tongue, and I did not allow God to take vengeance because I felt my revenge was better. The Bible states in Titus 3:2, *"They must not slander anyone and must avoid quarreling. Instead, they should be gentle and show true humility to everyone."* Proverbs 20:3 says, *"Avoiding a fight is a mark of honor, only fools insist on quarreling."*

So, Jesus, does this make me a fool? Things people say to me hurt and cause me to have rage and anger. What about them? Why do I have to change? How am I supposed to be okay when I'm blatantly being disrespected? I know it is hard to not be enraged but there is freedom from this angry spirit. I can tell you firsthand it is not the easiest spirit to deal with, and it is something you have to pray over constantly, lay at the feet of Christ, and allow the Holy Spirit to renew your mind. Ecclesiastes 7:9 states that we must control our temper, for our anger labels us a fool. The freedom in knowing that God has shown us the things we should take on when we have his Spirit. Galatians 5:22-24 says, *"But the Holy Spirit produces this kind of fruit in our lives: love, joy, peace, patience, kindness, goodness, faithfulness, gentleness, and self-control. There is no law against these things! Those who belong to Christ Jesus have nailed the passions and desires of their sinful nature to his cross and crucified them there."*

Utilize this time to write down some things that cause you to get upset, that cause you to have a straight attitude, that make you want to snap and go off.

Then pray:

"God, I come to You right now, laying all of my hostility and quarreling at Your feet. Please forgive me for my sins. Please forgive me for _____, _____, and _____. I do not want to be

labeled as a fool in Your sight but have Your mark of honor.
God, please restore in me. Restore love, joy, peace, patience,
kindness, goodness, faithfulness, and self-control. Allow Your
Holy Spirit to correct me and convict me when my flesh
tries to overtake me. Thank you in advance, Lord, for the
freedom You have given me to be a better me.
In Jesus' name, Amen."

Jealousy and Envy

For some women, jealousy and envy are two of the main reasons why a lot of women don't get along. Some struggle with other women being more successful, having more money, or even, of course, being with a better man. I personally struggled with jealousy and envy if a woman had a man I wanted. Jealousy and envy are synonyms, meaning being bitter toward someone or something you feel has an advantage, putting you at a disadvantage.

While attending my church, I thought I heard the Lord point out a particular rather handsome specimen, telling me that he was my husband. As if I really believed that. But why not? Why can't he be mine? He could sing, and I had always wanted a singer. He had a breathtaking smile, loved Jesus, and was living for Jesus, so it MUST be the Lord. Plus, I thought he was staring at me while he was singing for worship. I started to plot on this man.

I started researching, as women do. He was about to release a song and asked that his fans donate to him to help get the song off the ground. I was the first to donate and gave the most, almost half of what he received. We conversed, and he would tell me how he thanked God for me and that I was such a blessing.

I continued to feed what I thought was manifesting into my future and ignored all the red stop signs that Jesus was putting up. The man had just gotten out of relationship a year or so prior and clearly was still healing from that. He went out of his way to speak to me and even had a nickname for me. We exchanged phone numbers, and I thought God was doing an amazing thing. I waited for this person to tell me he felt the same way I did.

One day, I decided I needed to muster up the guts to tell this guy that I had the biggest crush on him. I told him I had my eye on him for a while and really liked him. His response was that he had brewing potential with someone he had just met. I was broken, confused, and angry with God that He gave me what I felt was a broken promise.

I had to find out who this so-called "brewing potential" was. I found her and had all the questions as to why. Why he chose her? What does she have that I don't have? Was she supporting him like I was? Not even close. She wasn't even living a Christian lifestyle. She went out to clubs, drank alcohol, and wore promiscuous clothing—not even close to the representation of a Godly wife.

One day, I received a text message from the guy that he was having a single release party. He included the flyer. At this point, I didn't want anything to do with him. He even started acting differently at church. My response was, "Wow, I'm so proud that you are finally releasing your song, and I'm sure it will be a great turnout. Congrats." He said, "Oh, you're coming, right? You have to. You were a huge part of why I am able to do this today."

So I opted in to go. But I had to make sure I was the finest thing that ever walked into that room. Not just to impress him but to show her and make my presence known. I saw her and cracked jokes. She had no rhythm, didn't know the words to his song, and wasn't even that cute in person. But guess what? She had the attention of the man I thought was made for me. I wanted that attention she had.

There were a number of things I did wrong. First, I didn't guard my heart, and that caused my anger toward God. Second, I was envious and jealous and talked down an individual I didn't even know. God had to show me all my pitfalls and downfalls as to why I don't and didn't have a husband. I struggled in that area.

1 Peter 2:1 states: *"So get rid of all evil behavior. Be done with all deceit, hypocrisy, jealousy, and all unkind speech."* Being envious and jealous of a human who has something or someone that doesn't belong to me to begin with is an evil behavior. Not only that, I was deceitful. I was deceiving a man that I wanted to be my husband into doing all the things a real supporter and a

wife would do, and I failed. It was, again, acting on my own accord of finding my husband and not allowing God to do what He does best and allow Him to find my husband.

I know for sure someone reading this has gone through something similar, and of course, we must pray and have God remove this evil behavior from us.

"God, I repent of any evil behavior of jealousy or envy. I was jealous when I didn't have ____, ____, and _____. I take these evil behaviors and pin them to your cross. Please help me to accept the things that are not for me, and only find joy in the things that You have already provided for me. Align my spirit that my only expectation is from You. In Jesus' Name. Amen."

Outbursts of Anger

I chose the college I went to because of a man I was head over heels for. I was completely naive, but no one could tell me anything. This man was my first real heartbreak, but a needed heartbreak. I did everything. I made sure his classes were intact. I wrote, typed, and edited some of his papers. I paid for video games and clothes. I gave this man everything I possibly could to prove to him that I was worth the risk. We got into petty arguments that generally occurred on Thursday nights, but we made up by Sunday, just so he could go out with his boys.

Everything was great until I found out he was talking, flirting, and hanging out with other women. That's right, I found out. I was a detective. I wasn't the type of girl who listened to what other people said. I liked to gather my evidence and present it to the suspect.

One day, I had had enough. He had a class on campus, and I made sure that I confronted him face to face. He had the nerve to tell me that he never loved me and didn't want to speak to me anymore.

I was furious. *You don't want to be with me after everything I have done for you?* I completely blacked out. I saw red, literally, and went off in front of his friends in the middle of the courtyard. I did not care.

What made my outburst worse was that he disclaimed me and acted like he didn't know who I was. That hurt to my core. But I acted like a complete nutcase. I had zero control over my emotions and allowed my anger to take full control. There was no remorse.

I was so broken, hurt, and depressed that I wanted to take vengeance. I definitely had resentment. I had given this man my all, everything. For what?

In Proverbs 27:3-4, it says, *"A stone is heavy and sand is weighty, but the resentment caused by a fool is even heavier. Anger is cruel, and wrath is like a flood, but jealousy is even more dangerous."* Often times, we don't look at the impact jealousy, envy, and anger has on the people in our lives or how it hurts us. It hinders us from blessings, blessing others, and being a light to others in a dark place. Better yet, it hinders you from being a Godly wife.

Ephesians 4:23-27 says, *"Instead, let the Spirit renew your thoughts and attitudes. Put on your new nature, created to be like God—truly righteous and holy. So stop telling lies. Let us tell our neighbors the truth, for we are all parts of the same body. And 'don't sin by letting anger control you.' Don't let the sun go down while you are still angry, for anger gives a foothold to the devil."*

God, I come to you right now, confessing that my anger has a strong hold on me. Sometimes I can control my anger without sin, and other times I can't. I lay all of these times _____ I was angry and I allowed my anger to take control. Please allow your spirit to renew my thoughts and create me to only be more like you and less of my flesh.
In Jesus' Name.

Selfish Ambition

Have you ever felt that if you reached a certain level of success that you would be able to get the man with money and the nice car? Do you ever speak boldly about Jesus so others will follow you instead of Christ? Do you ever gain a possession faster than another person after the same thing and throw it in her face instead of giving thanks to God and encouraging that person that they can do the same thing?

Too many times, as women, we tear each other down with the fierce competition of being the first and being the best. We never want to lend a hand to someone who needs help. We'd rather watch her suffer because we feel she doesn't deserve to win. We're selfish with our money, careers, cars, and homes as if we provided them to ourselves. We are not what God has created us to be: generous.

The Bible speaks to selfish ambition by giving an example. In James 3:15-16 it states, *"For jealousy and selfishness are not God's kind of wisdom, such things are earthly, unspiritual, and demonic. For wherever there is jealousy and selfish ambition, there you will find disorder and evil of every kind."*

For my birthday this year, I spent it with everyone at my local church. One young lady was having financial issues and car trouble and needed encouragement. The night before my birthday, she put in our group chat for our millennial group that she needed a ride to church and asked if anyone could help.

I heard God tell me, "Give her a ride." My flesh said, "Maybe someone else will be generous enough to give her a ride. It's my birthday." However, I made the choice to be obedient.

Before this encounter, I did not know who she was, but my husband and I gave her a ride to church. She even went to dinner with our millennial group. I didn't hear from her for a few weeks until she texted me. I reached out, scheduling a time we could meet and chat. Although I was on the opposite side of town, I picked her up, paid for lunch, and we talked for hours. She was in distress. Life had hit her hard, and it showed. But I gave her the love of God. I sat and talked with her until she understood all that the Holy Spirit told me to tell her. I provided rides for a good two months. Never did I knock her down, make fun of her because she didn't have an operable car, nor ask for gas money.

I decided to be generous. I followed the Spirit. I wasn't pressured and did it purely from my heart. In 2 Corinthians 9:7-8, the Scriptures read, *"You must each decide in your heart how much to give. And don't give reluctantly or in response to pressure. 'For God loves a person who gives cheerfully.' And God will generously provide all you need. Then you will always have everything you need and plenty left over to share with others."*

Generous does not always mean giving money. Being generous is a heart thing. I'm giving all I can from my heart to anyone in my environment who needs help. I would love for God to give to me from his heart. He told me He would generously provide everything I need.

Selfish ambition leads to destruction. No one ends up hurt but you. Always check your heart and your motives. Make sure they're not your fleshly motives but are pure. If this is your struggle area, write down all the ways you selfishly tried to accomplish something for yourself and no one else. List all the times you can remember when you could have helped one of your fellow women but chose not to because you were disobedient to God's small voice.

God, I come to you right now kneeling in forgiveness. Forgive my selfish desires and ambitions. Please fill me with generosity. Help me understand that no good thing that you have given me belongs to me and that it all comes from You. Help me notice others who are in need of You. Help me lead others to You, not because I want followers, but because I want them to be followers of You.
In Jesus' Name. Amen.

Drunkenness

Growing up, I was told that drinking alcohol was a sin. I believe that individuals who learned this taught behavior look at people who drink and love the Lord as if it were a sin. Drinking alcohol is not a sin. Nowhere in the Bible does it state that drinking alcohol is a sin. In fact, throughout the Bible, wine and alcohol are mentioned and used. Jesus turned water into wine. It is the abuse of alcohol and becoming drunk to a point where we have no control of things we say or do that are sins.

After consuming a great amount of liquor, we don't necessarily act as ourselves. We become distorted, out of place, belligerent. Our words are slurred, and we have trouble walking and driving. We utilize alcohol as a dependency when we feel that life has become more than difficult to bear.

We have seen in movies and television how women are supposed to act after finding out that their man has cheated or broken up with them, how we should react if we're suffering from past hurts from family, be it a parent or sibling, and even how we should numb ourselves if we've been sexually violated as child or even in our adult lives.

We drink away the misery of all the things we feel instead of allowing the Savior to come in and heal all the brokenness inside us. Ephesians 5:15-20 reads, *"So be careful how you live. Don't live like fools, but like those who are wise. Make the most of every opportunity in these evil days. Don't act thoughtlessly, but understand what the Lord wants you to do. Don't be drunk with wine, because that will ruin your life. Instead, be filled with the Holy Spirit, singing psalms and hymns and spiritual songs among yourselves, and making music to the Lord in your hearts. And give thanks for everything to God the Father in the name of our Lord Jesus Christ."*

I have learned from my walk with God that not everyone can do the same thing that others do, including other Christians. While in college, I had to make a choice to be obedient to what God has called me to do. I went to parties, drank alcohol, and even smoked marijuana—the whole college experience. This was a learned habit received from the guy I was dating at the time.

You know, the same one I completely went crazy in front of on my college campus. Because we had engaged sexually, our spirits were intertwined. I started to act like him but in a female version.

I remember a specific party in particular. It was my first fraternity Halloween party. Some friends came down from my hometown and, of course, we consumed a lot of alcohol. My ex-boyfriend never wanted to go to parties with me and always said he would see me there. At this particular time, we were working on the relationship because he had broken my trust. He wanted to work out our issues and focus on the relationship. I arrived at the party after him and saw him dancing with another girl. I wasn't the type of girl to get upset when her man danced with another female, but I did have a problem with him asking for her number in front of me. Intoxication, anger, and betrayal are definitely not a good mix.

I confronted him publicly once again. I told him that I was done and pushed him. The odd thing about this encounter was that it was the beginning of my night out and I wasn't going to allow him to be the center of my joy. I enjoyed my night, danced, and drank to drown out my thoughts of embarrassment. How naive I was for falling for the same sly words he pretty much said every time he was caught cheating. The pain may have subsided for that night, but the next morning I had to deal with the pain of how he made me feel.

I had to make a choice for the life I wanted to live. I decided that drinking alcohol was not for me. I may occasionally drink wine, but it wasn't too often. The conviction I felt every time I drank alcohol only brought memories of mistakes made while drinking. I had to seek the Father in the middle of my mess and allow Him to guide me to freedom.

Again, drinking alcohol is not a sin, but in prayer and supplication, ask God if He is pleased with your current consumption and if it hinders your light to bring people into His Kingdom.

God, please forgive me for using alcohol as a dependency when I should only be leaning and depending on You. Please show me and tell me clearly where my consumption of alcohol is beyond Your limit for me. I want to live a righteous life and be filled with Your Holy Spirit. I do not want my alcohol consumption to dim the light that You have given me as an example to those around. Convict me when I am wrong and correct me with your gentle unfailing love.
In Jesus' Name, Amen.

Wild Parties

Going to a party is not a sin. This is another subject instilled in us that going to the clubhouse or fraternity party is sinful.

Indeed, it is very incorrect. What is inside of those types of parties can cause us to sin or be around unnecessary danger.

I did most of my partying in high school. Most of my desire to go to parties ceased in the middle of my sophomore year in college. In high school, there was a party my brother and I were dying to attend. The two people throwing the party were popular, and their parties were always amazing. I believe this was the second or third party of theirs that I had attended. Their parties always took place in their basement.

At this party, two groups of women envied each other because two of their head leaders had relations with the same guy. Of course, the jealousy and the envy ended up in a fight. You could tell they were heavily under the influence of alcohol. They were escorted out, and we continued the party. About an hour later, when the party was almost over, there were gunshots. That's right—gunshots! A man was shooting at another man for dancing with his woman. At that point, the party was over because the police shut it down.

The next day after church, my uncle told us he had heard what happened at the party and said he was glad we were safe. He pressed upon us the importance of our surroundings no matter how much fun the environment is.

He was right. Knowing your surroundings is important. Knowing the environment that you choose to be around could create more probability for danger to arise. Is that the fun you want to have with your life, always being at a high risk? No doubt you can get shot anywhere and at any time, but be wise about your decisions.

If you noticed in the example above, it wasn't only the gunshots that brought danger to the party. It was the jealousy, the envy, the quarreling, the fighting, and the drunkenness. You see celebrities who show that living the fast life and being the life of party make it seem as if partying is the only type of fun you can have.

Romans 13:13-14 states, *"Because we belong to the day, we must live decent lives for all to see. Don't participate in the darkness of wild parties and drunkenness, or in sexual promiscuity and immoral living, or in quarreling and jealousy. Instead, clothe yourself with the presence of the Lord Jesus Christ. And don't let yourself think about ways to indulge your evil desires."* Being in those kinds of environments sparks your flesh to do things it doesn't normally do. Christians have fun, too. I say it jokingly but seriously, too. Once you find the right church that feeds your soul and spirit and keeps it full, become a part of the church. You create lasting friendships that help you to be more than you ever thought imaginable.

"Help me, God. I struggle in this area. I love the thrill of wild parties. Help me recognize the people I am surrounded by, and help me recognize my surroundings. Convict my spirit, oh God, and

take the desire to want to indulge in these dark places. Create in
me the desire of fun that You have for me. Please continue to strip
away my sinful nature, and place Your spirit there.
In Jesus' Name, Amen."

Maybe you don't struggle with any of the areas mentioned. You may not even stumble on any of these sins listed in Galatians 5:19. Continue to be the light that you are. Help those around you live righteous lives. If there is something you need to work on but have not been able to pinpoint where you fall short, pray Psalms 139: 23-24: *"Search me, O God, and know my heart; test me and know my anxious thoughts. Point out anything in me that offends you, and lead me along the path of everlasting life."*

We all have things we need to work on in our lives. We were born into sin. We are not made perfect. Only God is perfect. Although we may fall short of the glory of God, we still should strive to be more like him every day.

In the midst of your singleness, seek God and allow Him to mend you. Constantly pray over yourself. Allow God's conviction to stick to you and push you to change (Ephesians 4: 20-24).

Chapter 5

Date God

Rejection is a feeling we don't ever want to feel, especially from men. We also don't want to feel that we are not appreciated, loved, respected, or valued by someone we care about.

What determines our value? How do you value yourself? Is it when a man strokes your ego and says you are the most beautiful woman he has ever seen? Do you like the way he compliments your short dresses that show a little skin? Is it the good morning texts you receive every day? What about when all of that stops? Will you still feel valued, or will you feel that your value has lessened because of how one man has made you feel?

Sometimes we get caught in what society dictates how a woman should dress and look to be beautiful. We are taught the less clothing, the better, and to show off all goods we have inherited for the world to see. Celebrities worship changing their figure to make themselves more appealing to the eye. Celebrities and their platforms make you believe that injections and implants enhance your beauty on the outside but don't mention how it damages the inside. These chemicals we place in our bodies do more harm than good in order to have the center of attention.

Psalms 139:13-14 says, *"You made all the delicate, inner parts of my body and knit me together in my mother's womb. Thank you for making me so wonderfully complex! Your workmanship is marvelous—how well I know it."*

Sad to say, most of don't know how marvelous the Lord's workmanship is because we don't take the time to get to know who He is. We can't even grasp the thought that what the Lord has given us is enough because we are told from so many men that what we have is inadequate.

When I was rejected and stood up by different men, I was still actively a part of my local church. You know, a lukewarm Christian, half-saved, and the other half was my sinful nature. I was a part of a small group that had weekly Bible studies and outings. I had to get to know myself the way God knows me. I had to start to see myself the way God saw me, not the world. I had to date God. I had to know God's nature, and His thoughts toward me.

I spent so much time and energy on getting to know different men while maintaining my surfaced relationship with God. When you are in a relationship or dating, your full intention is getting to know that person by talking on the phone, dating, putting cute emoji's under their statuses, right? You are intrigued with what this individual has to say because of the intense interest you two now have.

We must take that same approach with God. How can you say you have a relationship with God, make an assumed opinion about who He is, but won't actually take the time to read about Him to know how thoughtful He is toward you? Is that a real, authentic, relationship with God? Absolutely not! Yet, we do it all the time and constantly put our hearts in a state of grief by allowing men to terrorize our hearts, damper our moods, fuel our independence, and lower our self-esteem and our confidence.

I met this guy online, and we decided to introduce ourselves at a local restaurant. Immediately, we had a "so-called connection." He paid for breakfast, and I skipped out on church that Sunday to spend the day getting to know him. All we did was watch movies, sleep, cuddle, and eat. Yes, all within the first few hours of knowing each other. He was a jokester, which came naturally to him. I was twenty-three years old, and he was thirty-nine. Surely, I was dealing with a man who knew what he wanted, right? He said all the right things. I received good-morning texts, follow-ups throughout the day, and hookups. One day he asked to borrow money, and I said no. From that day forward, it went left. Far left. Because I said no, I was a selfish brat, and no man would ever want to deal with a woman like me.

He said I needed to grow up and that I was immature. He said I needed to quit being so naive and stupid.

Soon after that, he became blatantly disrespectful. He yelled at me condescendingly, making sure I recognized who he was and that he was the one in authority. He told me I would never amount to anything due to my attitude. He thought he could teach me about life. I, of course, took offense to the hurtful things he said and started to question myself. Am I a brat? Am I immature? Is my attitude damaging my future? I stopped talking to him because I wasn't going to tolerate how he made me feel.

I stopped talking to him for a few months, and he did the whole "sweep-you-off-your-feet phase" and went right back to cursing me out. This time was different, though, because all the things he said didn't affect me any longer. Why? Because I knew how beautiful I was in Christ. I felt that God brought this man back into my presence for a short period of time to show me how strong and beautiful I was after being more acquainted with Him. My tolerance changed. I no longer allowed what I used to allow to dictate my mood, how I felt about myself, or what I thought about myself.

In Songs of Solomon 4, it talks about the beauty of the woman. I remember lying in bed in my 800-square-foot apartment, reading Songs of Solomon.

Songs of Solomon 4:1-12 says, *"You are beautiful, my darling, beautiful beyond words. Your eyes are like doves behind your veil.*

Your hair falls in waves, like a flock of goats winding down the slopes of Gilead. Your teeth are as white as sheep, recently shorn and freshly washed. Your smile is flawless, each tooth matched with its twin. Your lips are like scarlet ribbon; your mouth is inviting. Your cheeks are like rosy pomegranates behind your veil. Your neck is as beautiful as the tower of David, jeweled with the shields of a thousand heroes. Your breasts are like two fawns, twin fawns of a gazelle grazing among the lilies. Before the dawn breezes blow and the night shadows flee, I will hurry to the mountain of myrrh and to the hill of frankincense. You are altogether beautiful, my darling, beautiful in every way. Come with me from Lebanon, my bride, come down from Mount Amana, from the peaks of Senir and Hermon, where the lions have their dens and leopards live among the hills. You have captured my heart, my treasure, my bride. You hold it hostage with one glance of your eyes, with a single jewel of your necklace. Your love delights me, my treasure, my bride. Your love is better than wine, your perfume more fragrant than spices. Your lips are as sweet as nectar, my bride. Honey and mild are under your tongue. Your clothes are scented like the cedars of Lebanon. You are my private garden, my treasure, my bride, a secluded spring, a hidden fountain."

Jesus felt that way about little ol' me? Well, if Jesus felt that way about me, surely the husband He has for me will feel the same way.

That last time this man spoke to me crazy, I stopped him mid-sentence and said, "The words you describe are not the word the Lord says or thinks towards me. Therefore, I know that you are not the man that God wants for me." And I disconnected the call. I didn't get ruffled, my feelings weren't hurt. I was at peace with myself and with God.

At that point, I became confident with who I was in Christ. I will never allow a man to make me feel that I am less than what the Bible has called me to be. I will never allow a man to dictate the life I will have if it does not align with what the Word of God describes. And neither should you!

You are a bride, a treasure, a hidden fountain, a secluded spring. That's how valuable you are. Build your confidence in what the Lord has called you to be. Straighten your crown and walk in the boldness of Christ. You are more than a conqueror. You are the head and not the tail. You are above and not beneath. Any man that makes you feel less than that is not the man God has intended you to have. The man that God has for you is going to be a direct reflection of Songs of Solomon 4. You are everything God has told you that you are according to His word, and from this day forward, you will only walk in confidence. You will esteem yourself to the point where you will only expect the best because you are God's best. You will walk with discernment to know the difference between a fleshly date or a Godly mate.

Chapter 6

Hidden in Christ

To be hidden means to not be visible without looking. Songs of Solomon 4 refers to the woman being a treasure, a hidden fountain, and a hidden spring. In order to be found, you must be sought after to be found. Remember, he who finds a wife, finds a good thing. In order to be hidden in Christ, you must remain disciplined.

Three things essential with your walk in Christ are:

1. Being a part of a Bible-taught-based church,
2. Learning and staying in God's Word and developing a prayer life, and
3. Your worship life and how you worship is reflected both in private and publicly.

Church

Being single helps me hide securely in Christ. After a short five months in Atlanta, I was tired of being lukewarm. On the one hand, I loved Jesus, but I loved the attention of men on the other. I needed to make a choice to be all in with Christ.

In the middle of May 2015 while relaxing after work, in order to chase after Jesus fully, I decided to delete from my phone all the men who served no purpose. One particular night after church service, I started to have a fire and passion to get to know this man named Jesus and just how gracious He was.

I started off with devotionals that pinpointed certain things I struggled with. I was constantly in His word, learning about the different promises He had for me. I may not have applied them appropriately in my life then because I had my own selfish motives, but I started to go deeper in the Word and learn the importance of the Bible. The small group that I was a part of played a big role in keeping me engaged and accountable.

I used to go to church on Sunday, return home, and try to pursue Jesus and develop my relationship with Christ by myself. I always fell into my flesh because I did not understand the importance of community. So many times we hear that church people are messy or that we are church hurt but fail to see the importance in which God has on the community of those who are like-minded.

1 Corinthians 12:18-26 says, *"But our bodies have many parts, and God has put each part just where he wants it. How strange a body would be if it had only one part! Yes, there are many parts, but only one body. The Eye can never say to the hand, 'I don't need you.' The head can't say to the feet, 'I don't need you.' In fact, some parts of the body that seem weakest and least important are*

actually the most necessary. And the parts we regard as less honorable are those we clothe with the greatest care. So we carefully protect those parts that should not be seen, while the more honorable parts do not require this special care. So God has put the body together such that extra honor and care are given to those parts that have less dignity. This makes for harmony among the members, so that all the members care for each other. If one part suffers, all the parts suffer with it, and if one part is honored, all the parts are glad. All of you together are Christ's body, and each of you are a part of it."

In order to be able to live a holy life, in the body of Christ, you must have community. You are created to be in harmony with each other. You are designed to hold your brothers and sisters accountable. When they fall short, you must be that friend to pick them up.

Galatians 6:1 says, *"Dear brothers and sisters, if another believer is overcome by some sin, you who are Godly should gently and humbly help that person back onto the right path. And be careful not to fall into the same temptation yourself."* So if you see that your friend, sister, or brother has fallen off track or fallen short, it is your responsibility as a friend to bring them back to the cross to allow God to strengthen their spirit and weaken their flesh. Be of great encouragement to them of how to win in Christ.

I ended up changing from one great church to my current church. Although I learned a lot about myself and was able to grow in Christ, it just was not home for me. My current church, The Faith Center in Tucker, Georgia, has literally changed my life! My pastor and his wife truly love hard on the people of God. My husband and I have grown so much and have developed a servant heart. They have helped me develop a discipline to truly seek God's word in every area of my life.

Becoming involved in ministry is vitally important in your growth with Christ. It helps you bring lost souls back to Christ. I think it is very important to be able to meet people where they are and let them know that it is okay to want change and help them to be the best versions of themselves.

Serving is huge to Christ, but for some reason or another, we avoid it as Christians. The Bible speaks how important it is to be of service to others and unto God. Not only is it important, God says He will honor you. A lot of us like to lead without the willingness to serve others. That is what Christ calls us to do. Jesus says in Matthew 23:11-12, *"The greatest among you must be a servant. But those who exalt themselves will be humbled, and those who humble themselves will be exalted."*

Serving in my local church is something that I actually take joy in doing. I serve in two ministries and do anything that is asked of me by my leaders. It's something I do without complaint or agony because I'm not serving them. I am of service to God.

Colossians 3:23-25 says, *"Work willingly at whatever you do, as though you were working for the Lord rather than for people. Remember that the Lord will give you an inheritance as your reward, and that the Master you are serving is Christ. But if you do wrong, you will be paid back for the wrong you have done. For God has no favorites."*

We have to serve the Lord with happiness. If that means being a greeter when people come to service on Sundays, being a teacher to the children's ministry, or ushering people to their seats, do those works of service as if Jesus walked into the room. How would you serve God?

There are many references in the Bible of the importance of being of Christ and serving. In fact, in Matthew 20:26-28 and Mark 10:43-45, Jesus speaks the same text twice about serving. Matthew 20:28 says that, *"For even the Son of Man came not to be served but to serve others and to give his life as a ransom for many."*

It is our duty to serve others if we are called to be Christians and follow Jesus. Be focused on serving the Lord that the many desires you have are not thought of when you are serving the Lord. God knows you want the husband, the marriage, and the children. He has heard your prayers. Are you willing to not be distracted by what you can get from God to save the life of someone who needs to be freed from the bondage of sin?

God's Word and Prayer

Growing up, and even throughout college, I was the "touch the Bible on Sundays only girl." I know that is some of you, too. I knew of the Bible my whole life and could only quote "Jesus wept" and couldn't tell you where the verse was located. I did know the books of the Bible, from Genesis to Revelation, but could not tell you what was in any of them. I knew nothing about the depth of God's love, the fact that He will fight my battles for me, that He is a provider, and that He desires to be in relation with us.

So often we get angry and frustrated with God and his timing. We question God's ability to be able to provide for us. We'd rather run to our flesh and act on our own accord. There's so much that God has promised us.

When I first moved to Georgia, I felt like, all of a sudden, I just started knowing God's word. I really couldn't tell you at this time how the passion and burning desire started. I feel it had a lot do with the people with whom I surrounded myself.

With only two days in Georgia, I visited my cousin's church where I learned my first verse at a New Year's Eve church service. It was Jeremiah 29:11: *"For I know the plans I have for you,' says the LORD. 'They are plans for good and not for disaster, to give you a future and a hope.'"*

In 2015, that was a verse I heard over and over again. I heard it in sermons, I accidentally stumbled on it, and I read it in books.

That was how I knew God was speaking His Word directly to me, to help me understand that the plan He had for me was far more than what I could imagine.

The year 2015 was definitely a year in which I spent more time learning God's word than I ever had in the last twenty-two years in church. I held on to verses that kept me encouraged. My favorite chapter of the Bible at that time was John 15, specifically John 15:7, which says, *"But if you remain in me and my words remain in you, you may ask for anything you want, and it will be granted!"* Yes, that is in the Bible. It's real. You read it correctly, but you must remain in Him. That means stay connected, walk in relationship, and do not depart from Him. After I read that for the first time, it was like a spark illuminated inside me.

I got to know Christ more every day. In the mornings I read devotionals. I had Scriptures on my computer monitors to show God that I was remaining in Him. I may have been remaining in Him in order to receive what I asked Him to grant me, but God had better plans, of course.

At this point I started to change. I asked God for a husband, and He started to mold me into a wife. God renewed my mind and transformed me into a new person. I couldn't tolerate the sinful things anymore. I couldn't do what the average twenty-three-year-old did. I wasn't in the party scene. I didn't smoke or drink. My good time was hanging around Christ-like people and learning more and more about Christ every day. The next thing I knew, when I found myself in any kind of struggle, I quoted scripture. Whenever I worried that God wouldn't grant me my husband, I prayed:

"In your Word, God, you tell me, in Philippians 4:6-7, that I should not worry about anything but be prayerful about everything. Right now, I don't understand why I can't have a husband. I'm doing all the things that You have shown me. I go to church, I'm in Your Word, and I have let go of my sinful nature. Reading in Your scriptures, Lord, You said to tell You what I need and thank You for all that You have done. God, I want a husband, not any kind of husband, but the husband You want me to have. Thank you for allowing me to move from California to Atlanta with peace. Thank You for Your peace that surpasses all understanding. I pray that You give me Your peace so I can remain focused on You. Thank You for providing for me and having Your angels protect me from all harm and danger. God, please continue to help me be patient and await Your perfect timing for the one You have created for me. Amen."

I'm not saying that I always said this type of prayer with happiness in my heart. I said this prayer when I felt like giving up and reverting back to my flesh. I said this prayer when I was in desperation and disappointment as to why I couldn't have what I wanted on my time. I felt I had waited long enough.

Praying is extremely important. It's your one-on-one time with God, talking to Him and allowing Him to reveal things to you, as well. Praying changes things. It not only changes you but also your environment and the people who surround it. God wants to be in relation with you. It is one of His ultimate desires. He wants to show you the best version of yourselves.

In James 5: 16, He says, *"The earnest prayer of a righteous person has great power and produces wonderful results."* The things you ask or bring to God, whether it be in the need of healing from disease, healing from your past, or healing in your mind, if you earnestly pray in righteousness, your results will be delightful.

Prayer is not something you should only do publicly. Being in private, and again, having your one-on-one time with God is essential. Matthew 6:6-8 says, *"But when you pray, go away by yourself, shut the door behind you, and pray to your Father in private. Then your Father, who sees everything, will reward you. When you pray, don't babble on and on as the Gentiles do. They think their prayers are answered merely by repeating their words again and again. Don't be like them for your Father knows exactly what you need even before you ask Him!"*

God knows you desire a husband, especially if you have prayed time and time again. He knows what you need before you even ask. That does not necessarily mean that He will give you the husband you want. He will only give you the husband you need. You must first allow Christ to be in your heart.

Needs must be met before your husband finds you. You must work out your kinks, be hidden in Christ, and put away your sinful nature in order for God to be able to bless you with the husband He has for you. This husband saves you the trip of heartbreak, disappointment, and settlement for less than what you deserve. Have the correct posture in order to receive the true promises that God has for you. Having a prayer life and having God's word deposited inside of you shields you from the pain we allow our flesh to put us through.

Praise and Worship

I love to be in worship. Worship is one of my favorite things. I can be in worship all day while I'm at work, riding in the car, and even when I'm at home. I can't tell you where worship became one of my true centerpieces of love and adoration to the Lord. What I can tell you is that God comes into the room when you sing praises to His name and worship Him in song, in spirit, and in truth. It's an unexplainable feeling. The spirit can be so heavy that it brings you to your knees because you know you are not even close to being worthy of the things God has prepared for you. You cry real tears, for despite thinking of all the things He has protected you from and all the times you turned your back on Him, God was still right there. There were times I didn't know where my next meal was going to come from, but somehow, some way, He provided.

When I listen to music, it takes me to a place of gratitude and gratefulness. It is not only therapeutic for me, but God says in His Word that it is something He loves. Psalms, along with passages elsewhere throughout the Bible, sheds light on praising and worshipping God.

Psalms 47:1-11 says, *"Praise the Lord! How good to sing praises to our God! How delightful and how fitting! The Lord is rebuilding Jerusalem and bringing the exiles back to Israel. He heals the brokenhearted and bandages their wounds. He counts the stars and calls them all by name. How great is our Lord! His power is absolute! His understanding is beyond comprehension! The Lord supports the humble, but he brings the wicked down in to the dust. Sing out your thanks to the Lord; sing praises to our God with a harp. He covers the heavens with clouds, provides rain for the earth, and makes the grass grow in mountain pastures. He gives food to the wild animals and feeds the young ravens when they cry. He takes no pleasure in the strength of a horse or in human might. No, the Lord's delight is in those who fear him, those who put their hope in his unfailing love."*

The Lord is so gracious with His love. He cares about everyone and everything. You only get that reverence when you look over your life and all you can do is sing out to the Lord for His goodness. His unfailing love means it cannot fail you. You will always find love with Jesus. If you have ever called on God to get you out of a difficult situation and He brought you out, you have a reason to throw up your hands and worship Him. Having a posture of praise and worship not only shows your adoration toward God but sets you up to be used and blessed by God.

Being hidden in Christ means totally deserting your old self and taking on a new creation in Christ. To be hidden is to be treasured when found by the right one. When you are found by the right one, he should be able to join you in prayer, praise, and worship, and he should know the Bible. You both should be able to walk in relation with the Lord. He shouldn't deter you from serving in your church; he should be right there, serving next to you.

I want to save you from the many heartbroken moments I had to endure to get to this point. Let Jesus love you. Become hidden, so when He brings you the one you don't have to ask questions if it's him. You don't have to struggle with giving yourself away to men who put on a facade of someone they aren't in order to impress you. When you're hidden in Christ this allows you to know your value. Once you understand your value as a daughter of God, you don't allow men to place you as an option.

Chapter 7

Don't Worry, He'll Find You

Why, as women, do we try so hard to please men and fail to understand that we are the favor? What in our thinking makes us chase a dead end?

We ask over and over, "God, where is my Boaz." Focusing on the wrong things, like why we haven't received our great man, makes us lose sight of what God has called us to be. Just because He hasn't brought our husbands on our time doesn't negate the fact that God's timing is perfect.

We become comfortable and think that since we've been dating for a while that he should be "the one," yet we feel the relationship is not even remotely close to marriage and that, overall, it's unhealthy. I want to help re-direct your focus of why we should not worry about finding or having a man, and why it's important to center our focus on Christ because He already knows what we want.

I remember being in a relationship with the young male mentioned in Chapter 2, who was divorced with two children. I did my best to please him. I had to show him that I was everything he ever needed even if he didn't see it.

I can't remember why we had decided to exchange gifts, but I went all out. I bought his children outfits and Barbie dolls. I bought him Dolce & Gabanna cologne, along with a $300 watch. I had to show him how much I appreciated him and respected the fact he had children, and that I was serious about him. In return, I received a knock-off Michael Kors bag purchased from a guy on the street corner. When I told him the bag was fake, his response was, "I don't even buy my mother expensive gifts."

On one particular day, he called me because he was excited about a newer model used car he had just purchased. He drove all the way to my apartment to show it to me—not to show me the car, but to show me that he was back on top and in a better position than I was. He didn't have the car a full week before he totaled it while driving under the influence. There I was, acting like the wife of a man who refused to acknowledge me as his girl.

Since I was off the next day, I drove forty-five minutes to his job to take him to get a rental vehicle. I needed to show him I was all the woman he would ever need. I still ended up without him.

Sometimes we want to be the savior. If we can be there for them at a particular time, we will. We tell ourselves they will realize that we're everything they have ever needed.

The truth is, if he is not pursuing you, he is not for you. The benefits of a wife should only be given when a vow is made before God and papers are signed and documented by your county.

Stop allowing men to manipulate you into thinking that if you don't help, you are the most despicable person in the world. That man is the very person you should flee from. That same guy, every time I opted not to enable his shortcomings, expressed, "That's why we aren't official" and "That's why I couldn't marry you." All I could think was that I must prove otherwise. Yet, he didn't have a heart after God, his financial well-being was unstable, and his heart did not belong to me.

What kind of so-called man should I have to prove myself worthy of? Jesus should be the answer, but my answer was, "I will do anything to have a husband." If a man can't view you as the wife, he can't obtain favor with the Lord. From there, unfortunately, he is not for you. And that is okay. You have to be okay letting go.

Ruth and Boaz are such a pivotal story in the Bible to a lot of women who desire a husband. A lot of women forget a couple of things. First, Ruth was not focused on being or becoming a wife. Secondly, Boaz noticed her; she didn't notice him.

Ruth 2:1-7 reads, *"Now there was a wealthy and influential man in Bethlehem named Boaz, who was a relative of Naomi's husband Elimelech. One day Ruth the moabite said to Naomi, 'Let me go out into the harvest field to pick up the stalks of grain left behind by anyone who is kind enough to let me do it.' Naomi replied, 'All right, my daughter, go ahead.' So Ruth went out to gather grain behind the harvesters. And as it happened, she found herself working in a field that belonged to Boaz, the relative of her father-in-law, Elimelech. While she was there, Boaz arrived from Bethlehem and greeted the harvesters. 'The Lord be with you!' he said. 'The Lord bless you!' the harvesters replied. Then Boaz asked his foreman, "Who is that young woman over there? Who does she belong to?' And the foreman replied, 'She is the young woman from Moab who came back with Naomi.' She has been hard at work ever since, except for a few minutes rest in the shelter."*

Ruth in no way was putting herself out there to get a man. Nowhere did she say, "Let me work in this field so I can get my man." Ruth was, quite frankly, nowhere near worried about getting a husband because she had just been widowed. She already had the posture of a wife without trying to be noticed. She was focused on providing for herself and her family. Boaz saw Ruth hard at work without trying to grasp his attention. There was something about her posture, how she carried herself, and how she worked that made him focus on this unfamiliar yet drawing woman.

Sometimes, as women, we are so focused on getting men that we reach desperate measures to try to get their attention. We choose to wear low-cut shirts to show our cleavage. We choose to wear skintight clothing to reveal our curves, just so they know, as well as everybody else, that we have amazing bodies. We wear shorts shorter than short to alert that we have some jiggle and draw their attention. We want men to know we are the whole package when Jesus clarifies we are the whole package without showing explicit parts of our bodies that were created to give to our husbands.

1 Timothy 2:9-10 states, *"And I want women to be modest in their appearance. They should wear decent and appropriate clothing and not draw attention to themselves by the way they fix their hair or by wearing gold or pearls or expensive clothes. For women who claim to be devoted to God should make themselves attractive by the good things they do."*

Be a woman who is more than what meets the eye. Trust that God will give you a husband who is extremely attractive with all his clothes on and his whole body covered. Your desire should be that God gives you a husband who is not only attracted to your outside appearance. God will give you someone who wants to focus on chasing God with you. God will give you a husband who is attracted to the God he sees in you.

Rearrange your focus. Ask God what He wants you to do. Where He needs you to be. Allow Him to order your steps on the path He needs you to be on especially if you are nowhere near furthering the Kingdom of God. Develop your relationship with

God and believe that He will blow your mind, and He will do just that.

I'm not saying it will be easy because it will be the hardest thing you do. But the most rewarding. Living for God is not easy when we have spent the majority of our lives in our flesh. Living for God is hard when your sinful nature overpowers the spirit God has given you. It's difficult to live for God when society makes all the wrong things, wrong ways, and left turns more appealing and accessible than the right noble, just, rewarding, and abundant life God has promised to give us. God will give you the desires of your heart because He placed them there. You have to trust in Him and trust that His Word is true. We must be obedient to the voice of God and where He directs us, and at the same time, we must understand that He hears our requests. *"Those who live only to satisfy their own sinful nature will harvest decay and death from that sinful nature. But those who live to please the Spirit will harvest everlasting life from the Spirit. So let's not get tired of doing what is good. At just the right time we will reap a harvest of blessing if we don't give up"* (Galatians 6:8-9).

Don't worry about why the guy you may think you want doesn't give you the attention you want. If he doesn't call or text you, don't worry about it. If he is not pursuing you the way you expected, drop him. The man God has for you will point you out and pursue you. You won't have to ask for his time or attention. God will always supersede your expectations. You must put your complete trust in God and keep your focus there, trusting Him and His process.

Chapter 8

What Is a Godly Mate?

In July of 2014, I was in the middle of wedding plans. I thought I was supposed to get married right after I graduated from college. My boyfriend, Randy, was still in school and didn't have a job. I was forcing a time that was for the future because I wanted what I wanted right then and there. He wasn't in a position to be a married man. He couldn't provide for or protect me.

Randy had never taken me out on a date even though we were together for three years. I found myself quite frustrated throughout our relationship because he couldn't buy me gifts or take me out. I was aggravated because he wasn't interested in church or being spiritual. He knew God was real but couldn't quote one Scripture or sing a hymn. I drifted far away from God because it was like pulling teeth trying to get Randy to go to church. He gave me every excuse as to why he couldn't go—his stomach hurt, he had a headache, his eye hurt. Every excuse imaginable.

Shortly after I graduated from college, in May of 2014, we got engaged. Because I forced it. I forced Randy to propose to me when he was not ready. Our engagement lasted about three or four months. I was reaching dead ends with everything. I had just graduated college and was making minimum wage as a teller at a bank. We were living in two different cities after I had to move back home and live with my mom. I had no idea what I wanted to do with my future.

I broke up with Randy. I told him we weren't getting married and that we were not going to be together anymore. I said we shouldn't force something that was not meant to be. At the time, I was frustrated I could not have what I wanted and felt that Randy could not be the man I needed.

On Labor Day weekend, I went to my mother's friend's home in Atlanta. She held a high position at a corporation and told me to apply for a job at her company. At the time, I was living in California, where my family and friends were.

The day before Thanksgiving, I was offered the job in Atlanta. My start date was in January of 2015. I thought of it as my new beginning. I knew I was called to Atlanta for a reason but didn't know why. I took the faith that I had and moved to a city that I knew little to nothing about, leaving my family and friends, my failed engagement, my childhood, and my accomplishments.

For the first four to five months in Atlanta, I lost myself. I lost control of who I was. I was interested in men and finding a husband. I gave myself away to men not deserving or worthy in order to feel wanted. I was a Sunday saint who got the Word on Sunday and went back to the same sinful nature on Monday.

I spent countless hours crying out to God and my mom, asking, "Where is my husband? Why can't I be married? When will it happen? Why can't it happen now?" I had no interest in God's perfect timing although the whole time I was complaining He was preparing me for what I had asked for.

Yes, I know I said we shouldn't speak for a year until we figured things out but that didn't happen. Every couple of months, Randy texted and checked in on me, or I would find a reason to reach out to him. It's crazy how every time I cried out to God, "Where is my Husband," Randy showed up. I purposefully ignored the answer God was giving me because I was distracted by different men.

In October of 2015, Randy sent me a message on Facebook asking how I was. At that time, we hadn't spoken for a good three to five months. We caught up and talked a little bit, and I told him I was coming out to California for the holidays and that maybe we could go out to eat to catch up. He was so excited. He wanted to do something extravagant for me. He wanted to show me that the man he was when I left him was not the same man as he was then. He had a job and a car, and he had the confidence to show me that I was everything he had ever wanted.

When December came, he did just that. He brought gifts, and we ate at one of my favorite restaurants. That first night, he laid out all his feelings and how he had truly changed. He apologized for past relationships and his shortcomings. He told me that if he had another chance with me, it would be different.

Quite frankly, I wasn't sold. I thought he was talking a great game. I told him we should wait until December 2016. We should continue to grow separately and not be in communication. Although that broke him, he had to accept my decision.

The next morning, I was walking with my mom and my cousin, and my cousin asked if I was completely done with that man. "If you were over him, you would let him go. Since you are asking to wait another year, you might as well work it out."

That made my mind go crazy. I had things to think about. I didn't know if I should take a chance with this man again or if I should let him go. Stringing him along was not going to be favorable to my feelings or his.

In January of 2016, when I went back to Atlanta, I was sitting in my car and telephoned Randy. I said we should work it out, and he should move to Atlanta. He asked how soon I wanted him to leave, and I told him immediately. He said he couldn't just drop everything. He had a job and a car note, and that he was thinking about going back to school. He said he would start looking for jobs in the Atlanta area but couldn't abandon his car because he had bills and a car payment.

We began conversing every day. We started to do our own Bible studies over the phone, and he prayed for us and the things in our lives.

On January 21, 2016, Randy was involved in a car accident. His car was totaled, but he wasn't harmed. The day after the accident, he called and told me the verse he was looking over in 2 Timothy, as if he hadn't just been involved in a car accident. It made me feel that although he had lost his vehicle, Jesus was more important than a replaceable, materialistic object. After his accident we continued with our normal Bible study every day. He pursued Jesus.

Randy had said having a car payment was the main reason he was unable to move to Atlanta. But God quickly stepped in and that factor was removed due to the accident. When Randy made the decision to move, he struggled telling his family.

One day, he found a one-way flight to Atlanta, Georgia, for only $98. Although he didn't want to leave his family, he told them he would be moving soon.

On February 27, 2016, he boarded his flight and moved to Atlanta, Georgia.

He took a leap of faith, leaving his family, friends, and everything familiar to go to a place he did not know—except for me, of course. Three weeks after moving to Atlanta, he found a job.

What was different between this time and the last time? Instead of forcing my timetable and how things should go, it was more of a smooth process. Everything aligned perfectly, and everything was timed perfectly.

Did Randy have everything all together when he moved to Atlanta? No, not at all. Did he have all the money in the world? No, not at all. I knew Randy was the man God had for me based on God's actions on making things happen. I knew there was purpose. Out of all the men I tried to date, there were no stop signs, left turns, or inconsistencies.

He moved out to Atlanta in February of 2016 and we married in November 2016. The whole process leading up to marriage went smoothly. I did not have to force anything. God made big chess moves that made me move myself out of the way.

The man God has for you may not have all the things or status in life you want him to have. That's the beauty of your marriage and marrying young.

It took me a while to be aware that Randy was the husband God wanted for me. What really confirmed everything was when we, together, found our local church two months before we married. The same guy I had begged to attend church every Sunday chose the church we now attend, serves diligently, and enjoys it. He has the desire to be a man chasing after God's heart. He may not be where he feels he should be, but it is a huge difference from not wanting to go to church to being a full-blown servant of Christ.

Randy is my Godly mate because in Matthew 19:5 and Mark 10:7-9, it says, *"This explains why a man leaves his father and mother and is joined to his wife, and the two are united into one. Since they are no longer two but one, let no one split apart what God has joined together."* Randy left his family, his mother, father, and his brothers to join me in Atlanta.

There is a purpose for my marriage that I may not have fully discovered yet, but soon—very soon—it will be revealed.

How can you determine if your mate is the one God has for you? Allow the Bible to be your answer to all your questions. If your husband or date do not resemble or align with what the Bible says a husband should be, you should re-evaluate with whom you are entangled. We all fall short and we all sin, but in the midst of the shortcomings we face, where does God fit in?

It all depends on your relationship with God. How often are you in communication with Him in prayer? Are you fasting over this situation to allow God to make it crystal clear to you if the man you seek interest in is the Godly man God has for you? God will answer your prayers, but you must be ready for the answer. Clearing out what you eat, hear, and watch can help you detour to the direction God wants you take and the answer you need to hear. I can only give you practical steps as to what I did to determine that my husband was the man God created just for me. My process may be different than yours, but that is when you need to seek God the most.

Prayer

I briefly talked about prayer and God's Word in Chapter 6. I want to show you how to be specific with the prayer you want answered. As stated earlier, prayer is your direct communication with God. That is how you grow in relationship with Him.

Every time I started to entertain a new guy, I told God, "Show me if this is the man you have for me." Sure enough, I would literally crash into a large stop sign and my feelings would become hurt based on a prayer that I told God to reveal to me. Although God made His "NO" very easy for me to comprehend, I took God's "no" as a foreign language that I could not understand. It was clear that the men chasing me were not in His will for me.

Praying is what helped me realize how we have the most generous God who gives us chance after chance once we have made bad decisions. Praying is what gave me hope to understand that His best always exceeds my best. Praying is what made me trust the process and trust that He truly will give me the desires of my heart.

There are a couple of prayers that will help guide you in the right direction. Prayer for God to reveal, to remove, to heal, and to remain patient in this time of waiting.

We have all heard the saying that the truth hurts sometimes. Honestly, truth is needed in order for us to be able to break free from what has kept us in bondage from doing the work of the Lord. God's spirit is truth, and we need His truth to be able to make the right decisions for the future He has for us.

John 16:13-14 states, *"When the spirit of truth comes, he will guide you in all truth. He will not speak on his own, but will tell you what he has heard. He will tell you about the future. He will bring me glory by telling you whatever he receives from me."*

If you want to know if your current potential long-term mate is the one God has for you, pray this prayer:

God, I am coming to you because I need your guidance. I need your spirit of truth to reveal to me if ____ is the mate you have created just for me. If this is not the person you have designed for me, for your purpose, please remove him. Make the signs so clear that I can't deny that this is a sign from you. In this lesson, help me to be able to self-reflect on this lesson, grow from this teachable moment, and to better discern your spirit in the choices I make. Allow me to remain obedient to your voice and disconnect from this man who serves no purpose as a Godly mate no matter how much it hurts. May the pain I feel serve as a reminder that this is temporary and my best is nowhere near your best. Comfort me and heal my heart and redirect my focus back to You. Give me the patience to wait on your perfect timing. I don't want my timetable to prove itself better than Your timing because, again, Your timing is perfect. I know You will answer my heart's desire to be a wife. In the meantime, while I wait, perfect me in the ways that You see fit. In Jesus' name. Amen.

There were times I knew God was telling me that the man I dated was not the one. He showed me all the signs until I finally listened. My heart broke, but God comforted me and made me whole in Him. He began to show me in His Word how to remove the doubt, fear, and limitations I placed on Him regarding the husband I desired. He began to show me there was a purpose for all that He allowed me to go through. It was not just for my growth; it was to help His people, too.

I believe my sole purpose in writing this book is to let women know that their suffering, doubt, and fear are a part of the process. Your anger that your husband isn't already in your life is a part of the process. The fact that you are not perfect and have things to work on is a part of the process. Your struggle now is a testimony later. Once this season of lessons has passed, you will be able to help someone who has no direction as to where to turn.

Isaiah 53: 10-12 says, *"But it was the Lord's good plan to crush him and cause him grief. Yet when his life is made an offering for sin, he will have many descendants. He will enjoy a long life, and the Lord's good plan will prosper in his hands. When he sees all that is accomplished by his anguish, he will be satisfied. And because of his experience, my righteous servant will make it possible for many to be counted righteous, for he will bear all their sins. I will give him the honors of a victorious soldier, because he exposed himself to death. He was counted among the rebels. He bore the sins of many and interceded for rebels."*

In the midst of your feelings right now, find comfort in knowing that although you may feel defeated as if love isn't going to find you or that you have failed in many relationships, God's plan is to prosper you after you have suffered a little while. It will make the reward so much sweeter.

Fasting

Sometimes our minds are cluttered with the things we watch, things we hear, and even the things we eat. It makes it hard to hear clearly from God. We must cut out all the noise and consecrate ourselves unto the Lord. Fasting helps hear clearly what the Lord needs you to do. Fasting helps you receive direction from God. You can fast from anything that you feel deters your time spent with God.

It could be all forms of social media. Social media plays a huge part of our day-to-day lives. Many of us spend countless hours on social media but no time with God, and then we turn around and become upset because He hasn't answered our prayer for a husband.

You may battle with watching television. The new season of your favorite show or shows have started, and it takes you away from spending time with God. Then, all of a sudden, we feel as if God can't hear us and He is extremely far when we are the ones who created the division.

Eating was my problem. I loved chicken, French fries, and junk food. I struggled with giving up what I felt at the time was this amazing food. Growing up, in my hometown, fasting was not a normal thing that was practiced, and I was ignorant as to what the Word says about fasting.

After I moved to Atlanta in 2015, I briefly tried fasting at the beginning of the year with my cousin and her family. I ate no meat for the most part of January, not even on my birthday. I didn't like fasting because I didn't know the importance of it. I didn't know it brought clarity and insight as to what God was doing and going to do. I didn't know it teaches you to depend more on God. It teaches you to trust Him and the plan He has for you.

When it comes to fasting, the whole world, including social media, does not need to know what you are doing. You don't have to go to work looking like someone is depriving you of nutrients and that you absolutely have no energy. So many people send farewell warning statuses that they are going to disappear for a while because that is what God told them to do.

In my opinion, they miss the reward based on what the Word says.

Matthew 6:16-18 says, *"And when you fast, don't make it obvious, as the hypocrites do, for they try to look miserable and disheveled so people will admire them for their fasting. I tell you the truth, that is the only reward they will ever get. But when you fast, comb your hair and wash your face. Then no one will notice that you are fasting, except your Father, who knows what you do in private. And your Father, who sees everything, will reward you."*

The very thing you have been asking God for may be rewarded to you if you diligently seek Him while you are fasting. He may not hand the man of your dreams down on a cloud, but He will show you which path to take. You must trust Him.

Characteristics

Your Godly man is someone God gives you. It is not to say that you will not endure issues and problems in a relationship. However, the goal and the focus are different. A lot of us have our different lists of what we want in a man, but we choose to date someone who undermines our morals and values. We fail to see the man who truly pursues us, and we consider the guy "thirsty" when we chase after an unstable man.

What we Chase

1. **Inconsistency:** He claims he is interested and only wants you, but you hear from him once every other week. He blames that on being busy with family stuff, but he doesn't include you in the situation when you ask. He may always be out with his boys and never checks in, but his social media is always active. He is inconsistent with his life, jobs, communication, and decisions.

2. **Let's chill:** We like him because he gives us the attention in private that we have been seeking. Yet, you always find yourself at his home or he's at yours. He never wants to go out, and he blames that on being a homebody. Whenever you choose to indulge in your flesh, your spirit is convicted because you know the direction you want to go and where God is leading you, but sin is trying to stunt your growth.

3. **I ain't lookin' for a girl:** This is the guy the majority of us fall for. This guy seems to dot all your I's and cross all your T's. Everything about this man is great until you start talking about relationships. It seems as if he cringes at the fact that it is even a question. He is completely honest that he isn't looking to be in a committed relationship. He doesn't want to be committed but requires that you treat him as if he was already your husband. You buy things to impress him, cook for him, clean for him, engage in

intercourse just to prove to him that you are worthy enough to be committed to. All along, he has been seeing other women on the side, and although hurt, he feels you shouldn't be because he had told you, "I ain't lookin' for a girl."

4. **Lying is his best friend:** This is the man who lies to you from the very first time you have communication with him. He is the man who tells you that he loves Jesus and goes to church, but farther down the line, when it comes to Sundays, there is ALWAYS an excuse why he can't make it. He lies that his women friends are just friends, when your intuition tells you otherwise. He lies about where he is and what he is doing. We know he is lying blatantly to our face. He lies about having a job; he lies about how he lives; he lies about his finances and his credit score. We get in deep with this type of man and come out wondering why we are empty handed.

I am sure there are other characteristics I haven't named that we accept and chase after, but I chose the ones that the Holy Spirit wanted me to speak about. Unfortunately, we can't always blame the man in this case because he is a reflection of with whom we choose to spend our time, heart, and effort. If he can't hold a conversation with you and check on you every day, he is not pursuing you. Let him go. Completely.

Although intercourse is the furthest thing from your mind when he asks you to chill, it's the first thing on his mind. There has to be a boundary set when you are getting to know someone as your potential mate. If you have been dating for years and he doesn't want to take you out or allow you to meet his parents, you must evaluate what you are asking God to grant versus what you are settling for. Clearly, this can't be God's best for you.

It's fine if a man tells you he is not looking for a relationship. It is completely okay that he does not want a relationship. You must be able to know and accept that this man may never want the commitment you desire. In order to save your heart, time, money, and effort, ask questions upfront before your feelings become invested so it is easier to let go. Not just let go, but not entertain an individual who doesn't see the favor you carry.

Most importantly, if this man can't be honest with you about his relationship with Christ, what makes you think he will be honest with anything else? If you carry the Holy Spirit with you, you know the Holy Spirit is the Spirit of Truth. His lies should totally contradict what you stand for and believe in. God will give you someone you can talk and walk with in all truth.

Godly Mate Characteristics

1. **Man who chases after God's heart:** Acts 13:22 says, *"But God removed Saul and replaced him with David, a man about whom God said, 'I have found David son of Jesse, a man after*

my own heart. He will do everything I want him to do.'" A man who chases after God's heart may not have his relationship with Christ as strong as he desires it to be, but at least he has the desire to learn about Christ.

My husband knew nothing about Christ when we first met. He just knew that he existed. The man I met back in 2011 is a completely different man today. For that, I am grateful. It is beyond attractive to see a man know Jesus, read Scripture, and pray over you.

2. **Tither:** Yes, I am definitely going to speak on this because it is important. It is important for the men who state that they love God but don't give because of money-hungry preachers and churches. I allow the Word to speak for itself, no matter if the pastor, minister, or preacher is money hungry. The Word of God doesn't address that you shouldn't give to the money-hungry pastor. He says to not cheat Him.

Malachi 3: 8-10 is one of my favorite scriptures. It states, *"Should people cheat God? Yet you have cheated me! But you ask, 'What do you mean? When did we ever cheat you?' You have cheated me of the tithes and offerings due to me. You are under a curse for your whole nation has been cheating me. Bring all the tithes into the storehouse so there will be enough food in my Temple. If you do, 'says the Lord of Heaven's Armies,' I will open the windows of heaven for you. I*

will pour out a blessing so great you won't have enough
room to take it in! Try it! Put me to the test!"

There is something attractive about a man who has his finances prioritized. He knows he must honor God first. Men who honor God first eliminate the very root of why a lot of marriages end up in divorce: finances. While single, make sure you are honoring God in your giving.

3. **He is willing to wait:** That's right! He is willing to wait until your wedding night to have intercourse with you. I'm not saying it will be easy because we all have our weaknesses, but he is willing to wait. He understands the importance of loving you as you are and learning the innermost parts of your heart because we live in a world where sexual immorality is more common than only giving yourself to your husband.

Two Scriptures show us that intercourse is designed for marriage, and waiting before marriage is something that is biblical.

1 Thessalonians 4: 3-4 reads, *"God's will for you is to be holy, so stay away from all sexual sin. Then each of you will control his own body and live in holiness and honor."* It is in his will to abstain from sexual sin in order to honor him. When you are married, that's a whole different story.

Hebrews 13:4 says, *"Give honor to marriage, and remain faithful to one another in marriage. God will surely judge people who are immoral and those who commit adultery."*

I know for a fact that I will be facing the Lord's judgment because I was sexually immoral. My husband was willing to wait until we got married. We bought a blow-up bed so that he would be on the floor and I would be in my bed so we wouldn't be tempted. We may have slipped up a few times being sexually impure, but he was willing to wait because he wanted to honor the Lord with me. In the midst of our sex outside of marriage, I knew that he was the man God had for me because he wanted to learn about Jesus, become a part of church, and serve in the church.

4. **Never have to ask why, where, or who:** You don't have to ask where he is, or why he hasn't called, who this girl or that girl is, why he can't take you out publicly, why you can't meet his parents, or what his plans are because he makes that clear to you. A man of God who knows he is looking for a wife will be upfront and honest with his intentions. You don't have to guess or wonder. You will know. Taking you out is a pleasure for him because he can intellectually get to know the woman you are. He won't be ashamed to take you to dinner, movies, or on adventures.

You will be comfortable with the fact that everyone in his life isn't going to be male. You'll trust him enough to know that he won't mess up his favor for unfulfillment of his God-given purpose.

You will know this man is a Godly mate if he as closely as possible aligns with the Word of God. You will know that he is the one if you have prayed about it and have asked God to reveal, remove, and heal. What looks good on the outside may not be able to satisfy your insides.

Chapter 9

Kingdom Marriage

Marriages are supposed to be the closest thing people see to God. Although I'm still trying to figure it out and have only been married for about two years, people still come to me for marriage advice. As you read, I will tell you what I have struggled with thus far as a wife, what I've had to learn, and why marriage is important.

Being a wife is challenging. Our first year of marriage was a breeze, but this second year has been challenging. I have a submission issue that I am continually working on. I am very aggressive with my husband when it comes to obtaining goals in life. Whenever I feel they are unfulfilled or things remain stagnant for too long, I immediately express my frustrations to the point that my husband feels he cannot talk to me. I become dismissive and could care less about his decisions because he wasn't following Christ like I thought he should. Although he has grown tremendously, he still wasn't where I wanted him to be. I felt he was growing further and further away from Christ because his schedule changed and he had to work on Sundays. It messed up everything that we were working toward together.

One day, I got a hard knock on my head. We had one of our disagreements about what he was doing to lead our family. Later that night, I apologized for my tone. The next day when I went to work, I discovered he had created an online dating page. My heart sunk to the bottom of my chest because I didn't know what I had done to deserve this.

Later that evening when we both came home from work, I showed him what I had found. I didn't raise my voice or cuss him out. He told me all the things he was dealing with as a man. He felt as if he couldn't provide, that he was a failure, that he was not disciplined as a Godly man and was convicted every time he did the opposite of the Word of God. I told him, "In order for this to work, you need to contact our pastor." I said it with such a calm voice that I think it scared him. He spoke to our pastor, who then had a conversation with both of us.

Our pastor definitely checked me. Although there was no excuse for my husband's actions, I stressed him out with the pressure I put on him. The pastor was absolutely right! He said my husband felt he couldn't talk to me because of that pressure, and he was absolutely correct again. I put way too much pressure on my husband to get things moving in the right direction instead of being his helpmate.

I was called to be a helpmate. I was called to meet the needs of my husband and help him in the way he should go and to be able to submit to his decision as to where he leads us. Instead, I told him what he should be doing, how he should be doing it, and when it should be accomplished. I was the head of my household, and I was completely out of order.

This could have gone horribly bad if God wasn't in our marriage. I could have exploded, kicked him out, or even divorced him, but I recognized that our marriage still had purpose, and we would be able to help other marriages grow.

I had to learn how to forgive because he is not perfect. I, myself, am not perfect. I know that what he may struggle with could be my strength and vice versa. Was I upset? Yes, I was. At the same time, we needed to grow, and in order for us to be able to grow, we had to endure some turbulence. I'm grateful it was only a creation of a dating website and that he didn't actually talk to any women and had never physically cheated. However, he did challenge my trust. I look at our marriage as a direct reflection of our relationships with God. We sin, we aren't perfect, but God gives us another chance once we learn from the mistake.

Although I grew up in church, my husband was part of the unchurched. Yes, I married unequally yoked. My husband did not have the spiritual grounding that I did. He may have gone to church every so often with his family while he was growing up, but it was not consistent. He did not have the Holy Spirit upon him or in him. He has not even been baptized. I trusted that God had a greater plan for us to help those around us who weren't perfect but want to have the best marriage. God has purposed my husband and me to show other married couples that they can be young and still grow together. We have an assignment to teach wives that they can be the very reason why their husbands become saved.

1 Corinthians 7:13-14 says, *"And if a believing woman has a husband who is not a believer and he is willing to continue living with her, she must not leave him. For the believing wife brings holiness to her marriage and the believing husband brings holiness to his marriage. Otherwise, your children would not be holy, but now they are holy."*

If your husband may not be a fan of church or being the Godly man you desire, my dear wife, you must pray that he finds God and ask God to show you how to remain submissive while waiting. Holiness is attractive. If you live holy and are still submissive to your husband, he will change. You must be able to remain consistent. When small things change in your husband, celebrate those small wins so God can make those small wins turn into big ones.

That's what I had to do. I had to make Jesus attractive to my husband. I prayed and cried a lot. Two months before our wedding, we found our current church home, The Faith Center, in Tucker, Georgia. On our first visit, after experiencing the great worship and being fed with the Word, my then fiancé grabbed my hand and walked to the front to join. To this day, it is still the most amazing, rewarding decision we have ever made.

1 Corinthians 7:16-17 reads, *"Don't you wives realize that your husbands might be saved because of you? And don't you husbands realize that you wives might be saved because of you? Each of you should continue to live in whatever situation the Lord has placed you, and remain as you were when God first called you."*

The Lord knows not every marriage will start off as perfect as it should be, but don't lose hope. There is still purpose in the Kingdom of God for your marriage.

To my single ladies, enjoy your singlehood. Do not rush to the altar if you are truly not prepared for it. If you have kinks you need to work out, work on those before desiring to be a wife. Your marriage will not suffer as badly. For example, if you have jealousy and insecurities from a past relationship, it will do nothing but cause discourse between you both. You need to deal with those issues and release them. The enemy likes when you wiggle him into something God has ordained. You will find yourself mad and upset because he spoke to a woman in the grocery store. You should be able to walk into marriage with tools on how to fight the enemy, not how to invite him and destroy what God has joined together.

A kingdom marriage is designed to help other people win in their marriages, whether it be young or old. You can't help someone else win if you are bringing your past baggage with you. In marriage, you can't give up or walk out the door when he makes you angry. You can't make him sleep on the couch or in the other room like you see in movies. It drives separation, and that's exactly what the enemy wants. You can't drive to Mom's house or a friend's house, or even kick him out. You have to stay in it and fight.

There is no easy way out of a marriage when it's truly coveted by Christ. There are so many resources around us now that allow us to put our marriages back where they need to be. Because you feel he has made a mistake doesn't give you the opportunity to make the exact same one. Being in a relationship with someone is completely different than being in a marriage. It's not just a piece of paper. Being in a marriage is helping your mate find and live in his soul's purpose. It's his job, too. A kingdom marriage is rewarding because you are able to watch the life of your mate grow into something you didn't think was possible.

I'm not the perfect wife. I still make mistakes. The most important lesson I have learned is to take any anger or hurt I feel my husband has caused to the Father's feet in prayer. This is the most gratifying and comforting feeling you can have. Being a part of a supportive community of marriages and having great leaders to talk to when you fall short helps, as well. My husband and I will spend a lifetime together because God will always be the center, front, and back of what our marriage stands on.

Chapter 10

Win with the Godly Mate

Dating with your flesh makes you learn hard lessons. You are far away from God and even further away from becoming the person He has created you to be. Take the time to find out what you are really trying to have when it comes to desiring a husband.

If you know you are at a place where you have things in your life that you must fix, take the time and allow God to repair what you still struggle with. You must be able to be transparent with God in order to see your life transform.

Romans 12:2 says, *"Don't copy the behavior and customs of this world, but let God transform you into a new person by changing the way you think. Then you will learn to know God's will for you, which is good and pleasing and perfect."*

You desire the husband. Stop chasing and looking for him, sis. That is not in the will of God for you. I know you see the vision of yourself in a wedding dress and married with children. I know you see your happy ending. You will get it.

Habakuk 2:3 says, *"This vision is for a future time. It describes the end, and it will be fulfilled. If it seems slow in coming, wait patiently, for it will surely take place. It will not be delayed. God wouldn't give you a vision he doesn't plan on fulfilling for you."*

Make sure that, in the meantime, you find out what you really and truly desire from a man sent from God before He delivers him to you. Write it down clearly so God can fulfill your need. If rejection comes along your journey, it is God blocking you from a dead stop in your life. There is nothing wrong with you. You are fearfully and wonderfully made.

Show God that He comes first and that you can be obedient before what you are asking from Him is granted to you. Be all in with Jesus because His love runs deeply for you. He wants you to win in this life. I do, as well. Forget what the world says, and focus on what God says. What joy has the world brought you? Start to develop a closer relationship with Christ and experience His love, grace, and mercy. Allow His word to transform you into the being He wants to glorify His kingdom.

About the Author

Mary Lee Vance is a woman on a mission to help women around the world increase their self-esteem by reading the Word of God and releasing negative feelings from the words of man. She is dedicated to helping women live their lives in freedom.

Mary's convincing yet compassionate delivery style attracts women who want to live for Christ but are still battling with their sinful nature.

With the wisdom she has received from God, Mary exposes the truth about relationships by being transparent in her own life experiences, explains why we connect with the wrong men, and where the true change needs to start—with yourself. Once change happens, you can position yourself with the posture of God's best.